# Dress-Up Fashions™
## for 18" Dolls

## General Information

Many of the products used in this pattern book can be purchased from local craft, fabric and variety stores.

## Contents

# Party Set

DESIGNS BY **FRANCES HUGHES**

## SKILL LEVEL

EASY

## FINISHED SIZE
Fits 18-inch fashion doll

## MATERIALS
- Medium (worsted) weight yarn:
  5¼ oz/263 yds/149g burgundy
- Trendsetter Cha Cha chunky
  (bulky) weight yarn (66 yds/
  100g per ball):
  1 ball #224 wine
- Size E/4/3.5mm crochet hook
  or size needed to obtain gauge
- Sewing needle
- 3 small snaps
- 1½-inch hair clip
- Ribbon:
  ¼-inch wide: 2 yds wine
- 18-inch doll
- Wine sewing thread
- Stitch marker

## GAUGE
**Medium worsted burgundy:** 4 dc = 1 inch;
2 dc rows and 2 sc rows = 1¼ inches

## SPECIAL INSTRUCTIONS
Ruffles are made using 2 yarns. Use burgundy
for crochet stitches and wine held at back of
work to form ruffles. Insert hook in stitch and
into slot at top edge of wine at same time, yo,
pull through Wine, then through burgundy.
wine must be cut at end of each row it is used
on. The edges of this yarn must be hemmed by
folding two blocks of slots together to hide raw
edges at beginning and end of each row.

## PATTERN NOTES
Join with slip stitch as indicated unless
otherwise stated.

Chain-3 at beginning of row or round counts as first double crochet unless otherwise stated.

## SPECIAL STITCH
**Picot:** Ch 3, sl st in top of last st made.

## INSTRUCTIONS
## GOWN
**Row 1:** Starting at bottom of Gown, with burgundy, ch 54, dc in 4th ch from hook (*first 3 chs count as first dc*) and in each ch across. (*52 dc*)

**Row 2: Fold hem of wine** (*see Special Instructions*), hold wine at back of work, ch 1, sc in each st across according to Special Instructions, turn, cut wine with extra length for hem and fold hem. (*52 sc*)

**Row 3:** With burgundy only, **ch 3** (*see Pattern Notes*), dc in each st across, turn.

**Rows 4–23:** [Rep rows 2 and 3 alternately] 10 times.

**Row 24:** Rep row 2.

**Row 25:** With burgundy only, ch 3, dc in each of next 2 sts, [**dc dec** (*see Stitch Guide*) in next 2 sts, dc in each of next 3 sts] 9 times, dc dec in next 2 sts, dc in each of last 2 sts, turn. (*42 dc*)

**Rows 26–31:** [Rep rows 2 and 3 alternately] 3 times. (*15 rows of ruffles at this point*)

## BODICE
**Rows 1–4:** With burgundy only, ch 1, sc in each st across, turn.

## FIRST BACK
**Row 1:** Ch 1, sc in each of first 10 sts, leaving rem sts unworked, turn. (*10 sc*)

**Rows 2–6:** Ch 1, sc in each st across, turn.

**Row 7:** Ch 1, sc in each of first 6 sts, leaving rem sts unworked for neck opening, turn. (*6 sc*)

**Rows 8 & 9:** Ch 1, sc in each st across, turn. Fasten off at end of last row.

## CENTER
**Row 1:** Sk next st on Bodice, join burgundy with sc in next st, sc in next 19 sts, leaving rem sts unworked, turn. (*20 sc*)

**Rows 2–8:** Ch 1, sc in each st across, turn.

## FIRST SHOULDER
**Row 1:** Sc in each of first 6 sts, leaving rem sts unworked, turn. (*6 sc*)

**Rows 2 & 3:** Ch 1, sc in each st across, turn. Fasten off at end of last row.

## 2ND SHOULDER
**Row 1:** Sk next 8 sts of last row of Center, join burgundy with sc in next st, sc in each of last 5 sts, turn.

**Rows 2 & 3:** Ch 1, sc in each st across, turn. Fasten off at end of last row.

## 2ND BACK
**Row 1:** Sk next st on last row of Bodice, join burgundy with sc in next st, sc in each st across, turn. (*10 sc*)

**Rows 2–6:** Ch 1, sc in each st across, turn.

**Row 7:** Sl st in each of first 5 sts, ch 1, sc in same st as last sl st and in each st across, turn. (*6 sc*)

**Rows 8 & 9:** Ch 1, sc in each st across, turn. Fasten off at end of last row.

Sew shoulder seams.

## SLEEVES
**Rnd 1:** With WS facing, working around 1 armhole, join burgundy at bottom of armhole with a sc, evenly sp sc around, **join** (*see Pattern Notes*) in beg sc.

**Rnd 2:** Holding wine at back of work, ch 1, sc in each st around, working ruffle according to Special Instructions, join in beg sc. Fasten off.

Rep on other armhole opening.

## NECK TRIM

**Row 1:** With RS facing, join burgundy with sc at top left neck edge, evenly sp sc across to top right neck edge, turn.

**Row 2:** Ch 1, holding wine behind work, sc in each st across, working ruffle according to Special Instructions. Fasten off.

## FINISHING

**1.** Sew 3 snaps evenly sp down back opening.

**2.** With 18 inches of ¼-inch ribbon, tie bow in center of ribbon, leaving long ends for streamers. Sew bow to waist at center front of Gown above ruffles.

**3.** Tie 2 pieces 12-inch ribbon into bows. Sew 1 bow to top of each shoulder next to Sleeve ruffle.

## PURSE

*Note: Do not join or turn rnds. Mark first st of each rnd.*

**Rnd 1:** With burgundy, ch 3, join in beg ch to form ring, 6 sc in ring, **do not join**. *(6 sc)*

**Rnd 2:** 2 sc in each st around. *(12 sc)*

**Rnd 3:** [2 sc in next st, sc in next st] around. *(18 sc)*

**Rnd 4:** [2 sc in next st, sc in each of next 2 sts] around. *(24 sc)*

**Rnds 5–10:** Sc in each st around.

**Rnd 11:** Holding wine behind burgundy, work ruffle according to Special Instructions. Fasten off wine.

**Rnd 12:** Ch 4 *(counts as first dc and ch-1 sp)*, sk next st, [dc in next st, ch 1, sk next st] around, join in 3rd ch of beg ch-4. *(12 dc, 12 ch sps)*

**Rnd 13:** Ch 1, sc in first st, **picot** *(see Special Stitch)*, sc in next ch-1 sp, [sc in next dc, picot, sc in next ch-1 sp] around, join in beg sc. Fasten off.

## FINISHING

**1.** Cut 2 pieces ribbon each 9 inches long. Starting at one side, weave ends of 1 ribbon piece through ch sps of row 11 through to other side of Purse. Tie ribbon ends into a knot. Rep with other ribbon piece on opposite side of Purse.

**2.** Pull ribbons to close Purse.

## HAIR BOW

**Row 1:** With burgundy, ch 2, 3 sc in 2nd ch from hook, turn. *(3 sc)*

**Row 2:** Ch 1, sc in each st across, turn.

**Row 3:** Ch 1, 2 sc in first st, sc in next st, 2 sc in last st. *(5 sc)*

Rep row 2 until piece measures 18 inches from beginning.

**Last row:** Ch 1, **sc dec** *(see Stitch Guide)* in first 2 sts, sc in next st, sc dec in last 2 sts, Fasten off.

Fold into a bow and attach to doll's hair with hair clip. ∎

# Sweet Dreams

DESIGNS BY **SUE CHILDRESS**

EASY

## FINISHED SIZE
Fits 18-inch fashion doll

## MATERIALS
- Plymouth Yarns Dreambaby Shine light (light worsted) weight yarn (1¾ oz/160 yds/50g per ball): 3 balls each #119 pink
- Bulky (chunky) weight yarn: 5¼ oz/198 yds/150g pink
- Sizes G/6/4mm and J/10/6mm crochet hooks or size needed to obtain gauge
- Sewing needle
- 18-inch doll
- 12 ribbon roses with leaves
- 4 snaps
- Pink sewing thread

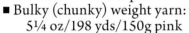
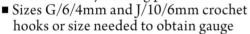

## GAUGE
**With light worsted yarn:** 5 dc = 1 inch; 2 dc rows = 1 inch

## PATTERN NOTES
Join with slip stitch as indicated unless otherwise stated.

Chain-2 at beginning of row or round counts as first half double crochet unless otherwise stated.

Chain-3 at beginning of row or round counts as first double crochet unless otherwise stated.

## SPECIAL STITCHES
**Shell:** (2 dc, ch 1, 2 dc) in indicated place.

**Double shell:** (2 dc, {ch 1, 2 dc} twice) in next st.

## INSTRUCTIONS
### GOWN

**Row 1 (RS):** With size G hook and light worsted yarn, ch 34, sc in 2nd ch from hook and in each ch across, turn. *(33 sc)*

**Row 2:** **Ch 2** *(see Pattern Notes)*, hdc in same st, [hdc in each of next 3 sts, 2 hdc in next st] across, turn. *(42 hdc)*

**Row 3:** **Ch 3** *(see Pattern Notes)*, dc in same st as beg ch-3, [sk next 2 sts, **shell** *(see Special Stitches)* in next st] across to last 2 sts, sk next st, 2 dc in last st, turn. *(13 shells, 4 dc)*

**Row 4:** Ch 3, dc in next st, [3 dc in ch sp of next shell, 2 dc in sp between next shells] across to last shell, 3 dc in sp of last shell, dc in each of last 2 sts, turn. *(67 dc)*

**Row 5:** Ch 3, dc in next st, sk next st, shell in next st, sk next st, dc in each of next 2 sts, sk next st, [**double shell** *(see Special Stitches)* in next st, sk next 4 sts] 3 times, double shell in next st, sk next st, dc in each of next 2 sts, [sk next st, shell in next st, sk next st, dc in each of next 2 sts] 3 times, sk next st, [double shell in next st, sk next 4 sts] 3 times, double stitch in next st, sk next st, dc in each of next 2 sts, sk next st, shell in next st, sk next st, dc in each of last 2 sts, turn. *(16 dc, 8 double shells, 5 shells)*

**Row 6:** Ch 3, dc in next st, shell in ch sp of next shell, sk next 2 dc of same shell, dc in each of next 2 sts, for **sleeve,** ch 4, sk next 4 double shells, dc in each of next 2 sts, [shell in ch sp of next shell, sk next 2 dc of same shell, dc in each of next 2 sts] 3 times, for **sleeve,** ch 4, sk next 4 double shells, dc in each of next 2 sts, shell in ch sp of next shell, sk next 2 dc of same shell, dc in each of last 2 sts, turn. *(16 dc, 5 shells)*

**Row 7:** Ch 3, dc in each st and in each ch across, turn. *(49 dc)*

**Row 8:** Ch 3, dc in same st, [sk next st, (dc, sc) in next st] across, turn. *(50 sts)*

**Row 9:** Ch 3, dc in same st, 2 dc in each sc across, ending with 2 dc in last st, turn. *(50 dc)*

**Rows 10–31:** [Rep rows 8 and 9 alternately] 11 times. **Do not turn** at end of last row.

**Rnd 32:** Now working in rnds, ch 2, 2 hdc in end of each row across, working in starting ch on opposite side of row 1, sc in first ch, [ch 2, sc in next ch] across, 2 hdc in end of each row across, hdc in each st across, **join** *(see Pattern Notes)* in 2nd ch of beg ch-2. Fasten off.

**Row 33:** Now working in rows, join in st at top left corner at base of neck, ch 3, dc in each st across, working across bottom edge, 5 dc in first st, sk next st, sc in next st, sk next st, [5 dc in next st, sk next st, sc in next st, sk next st] across to sts at ends of rows, 5 sc in first st, [sk next st, sc in next st, sk next st, 5 sc in next st] across, sl st in next st at base of neck edge. Fasten off.

Starting at 5-dc group below neck, sew 8 ribbon roses on every other 5-dc group spaced down right front.

Sew 1 side of 4 snaps evenly sp down WS of right front behind top 6 5-dc groups; sew opposite side of snaps down RS of left front opposite first side of snaps.

Sew lower right front slightly overlapping left front edge.

## SLIPPER
### MAKE 2.
**Rnd 1:** With J hook and 2 strands light worsted yarn held tog, ch 6, 2 hdc in 3rd ch from hook (*first ch-2 counts as first hdc*), hdc in each of next 2 chs, 5 dc in last ch, working on opposite side of ch, hdc in each of next 2 chs, hdc in same ch as first hdc, join in 2nd ch of beg ch-2. (*8 hdc, 5 dc*)

**Rnd 2:** (Sl st, ch 1, 2 sc) in next st, (*new beg of rnd*), sc in each of next 3 sts, 2 dc in each of next 2 sts, 3 dc in next st, dc in each of next 2 sts, sc in each of next 3 sts, 2 sc in last st, join in beg sc. (*11 dc, 10 sc*)

**Rnd 3:** Ch 2, hdc in each of next 7 sts, [**dc dec** (*see Stitch Guide*) in next 2 sts] 4 times, hdc in each of last 5 sts, join in 2nd ch of beg ch-2. (*13 hdc, 4 dc*)

**Rnd 4:** Ch 2, hdc in each of next 6 sts, [dc dec in next 2 sts] 3 times, dc in each of last 4 sts, join in 2nd ch of beg ch-2. (*11 hdc, 3 dc*)

**Rnd 5:** Ch 1, sc in each of first 4 sts, [sk next st, sc in next st] 3 times, sc in each of last 4 sts, join in beg sc. (*11 sc*)

Sew 1 ribbon rose to each toe.

## ROBE
**Row 1:** With size J hook and 1 strand each light worsted yarn and bulky yarn held tog, ch 33, dc in 4th ch from hook (*first 3 chs count as first dc*) and each ch across, turn. (*31 dc*)

**Rows 2–4:** Ch 3, dc in each st across, turn.

**Row 5:** Ch 3, dc in each of next 22 sts, leaving rem sts unworked for **armhole**, turn. (*23 dc*)

**Row 6:** For **shoulder**, ch 10, dc in 4th ch from hook (*first 3 chs count as first dc*) and in each of next 6 chs, dc in next 23 sts, turn. (*31 dc*)

**Rows 7–12:** Ch 3, dc in each st across, turn.

**Row 13:** Rep row 5.

**Row 14:** Rep row 6.

**Rows 15–17:** Ch 3, dc in each st across, turn. Fasten off at end of last row.

Fold each side to front, matching edge of armholes on each side.

Sew 1 inch above each armhole tog for shoulders.

## EDGING
**Rnd 1:** With J hook and 1 strand each light worsted yarn and bulky yarn held tog, join with sc in top left corner, evenly spacing sts so piece lies flat, sc around entire outside edge, join in beg sc.

**Row 2:** Now working in rows around sides and bottom edges, ch 1, sc in first st, [sk next st, 5 dc in next st, sk next st, sc in next st] around to top right corner. Fasten off.

Fold each top corner back to form lapel and tack in place. Sew 1 ribbon rose to each lapel. ■

# School Days

DESIGNS BY **SUE CHILDRESS**

## SKILL LEVEL

EASY

## FINISHED SIZE
Fits 18-inch fashion doll

## MATERIALS
- Fine (sport) weight cotton yarn: 3½ oz/350 yds/100g green variegated 1¾ oz/175 yds/50g each yellow, red and green
- Size F/5/3.75mm crochet hook or size needed to obtain gauge
- Sewing needle
- 18-inch doll
- 6 novelty heart buttons
- 3 round hook-and-loop fasteners
- Matching sewing thread
- Stitch marker

## GAUGE
4 hdc = 1 inch; 5 hdc rows = 2¼ inches

## PATTERN NOTES
Join with slip stitch as indicated unless otherwise stated.

Chain-2 at beginning of row or round counts as first half double crochet unless otherwise stated.

Chain-3 at beginning of row or round counts as first double crochet unless otherwise stated.

## SPECIAL STITCH
**Shell:** (2 dc, ch 2, 2 dc) in designated place.

## INSTRUCTIONS
### DRESS
**Row 1:** With variegated, ch 28, sc in 2nd ch from hook and in each ch across, turn. (*27 sc*)

**Row 2: Ch 2** (see Pattern Notes), hdc in same st, hdc in each of next 2 sts, [2 hdc in next st, hdc in each of next 2 sts] across, turn. *(36 hdc)*

**Row 3:** Ch 2, hdc in same st, hdc in each of next 7 sts, [2 hdc in next st, hdc in each of next 3 sts] across, turn. *(44 hdc)*

**Row 4:** Ch 2, hdc in each of next 3 sts, [2 hdc in next st, hdc in each of next 4 sts] across, turn. *(52 hdc)*

**Row 5:** Ch 2, hdc in each of next 4 sts, [2 hdc in next st, hdc in each of next 5 sts] 7 times, 2 hdc in next st, hdc in each of last 4 sts, turn. *(60 hdc)*

**Row 6:** Ch 2, hdc in each of next 3 sts, [2 hdc in next st, hdc in each of next 6 sts] across, turn. *(68 hdc)*

**Row 7:** Ch 2, hdc in each of next 4 sts, [2 hdc in next st, hdc in each of next 7 sts] 7 times, 2 hdc in next st, hdc in each of last 6 sts, turn. *(76 hdc)*

**Row 8:** Ch 2, hdc in each of next 10 sts, for **armhole**, ch 8, sk next 16 sts, hdc in each of next 22 sts, for **armhole**, ch 8, sk next 16 sts, hdc in each of last 11 sts, turn. *(44 hdc, 16 chs)*

**Row 9:** Ch 2, hdc in each st and in each ch across, turn. *(60 hdc)*

**Rows 10–14:** Ch 2, hdc in each st across, turn.

**Row 15:** Working in **back lps** (see Stitch Guide), **ch 3** (see Pattern Notes), dc in same st, 2 dc in each st across, **do not turn.** *(120 dc)*

**Row 16:** Ch 1, 2 sc in end of each row across to neck edge, turn. *(30 sc)*

**Row 17:** Ch 1, sc in each st across to waist edge, sl st in top of last dc on row 15, working across opposite side of back, [2 sc in each of next 2 rows, for **buttonhole**, ch 2, sk next row] 5 times, sc in first st on neck edge, turn. *(21 sc, 10 chs on buttonhole edge)*

**Row 18:** Ch 1, sc in each st and in each ch across, sl st in first st of row 15. *(31 sc)*

**Rnd 19:** Now working in rnds in back lps, ch 3, dc in each st of row 15 around, **join** *(see Pattern Notes)* in 3rd ch of beg ch-3.

**Rnds 20–28:** Working in back lps, ch 3, dc in each st around, join in 3rd ch of beg ch-3. Fasten off at end of last rnd.

**Rnd 29:** Join green with sc in first st, sk next 2 sts, 7 dc in next st, sk next 2 sts, [sc in next st, sk next 2 sts, 7 dc in next st, sk next 2 sts] around, join in beg sc. Fasten off.

Sew 5 buttons down left back opening opposite buttonholes on right back.

## SLEEVES
**Rnd 1:** Join variegated at center bottom of 1 armhole, ch 2, evenly sp 28 more hdc around armhole, join in 2nd ch of beg ch-2. *(29 hdc)*

**Rnds 2 & 3:** Ch 2, hdc in each st around, join in 2nd ch of beg ch-2.

**Rnds 4 & 5:** Ch 1, sc in each st around, join in beg sc. Fasten off at end of last row.

Rep on other armhole.

## TIE
Make 3 ch lengths each 100 chs long, leaving 1 inch of yarn at each end. Braid 3 lengths tog, beg and ending at ch ends. Tie yarn ends at each end of tie in an overhand knot to make fringe.

Place around Dress with ends in front; tie into knot to secure.

## PANTIES
**Row 1:** With yellow, ch 55, hdc in 3rd ch from hook and in each ch across, turn. *(54 hdc)*

**Rows 2–12:** Ch 2, hdc in each st across, turn. Fasten off at end of last row.

## CROTCH
**Row 1:** Sl st in each of first 21 sts, ch 2, hdc in each of next 13 sts leaving rem sts unworked, turn. *(14 hdc)*

**Rows 2–9:** Ch 2, hdc in each st across, turn. Fasten off at end of last row.

Fold each side of Panties above last row of crotch so right side overlaps left side ½ inch at center. Sew in place across lower edge. Sew 3 hook-and-loop fasteners evenly spaced down back edge.

## LEGS
**Rnd 1:** Join yellow with sc in first row on Crotch, 5 hdc in end of next row, [sc in end of next row, 5 hdc in end of next row] 3 times, [hdc in next st, sk next row, 5 hdc in next st, sk next row] evenly sp around leg opening, sk last st or 2 as needed, join in beg sc. Fasten off.

Rep on other leg opening.

## CAPE
**Row 1:** With green, ch 34, hdc in 3rd ch from hook and in each ch across, turn. *(33 hdc)*

**Row 2:** Ch 3, dc in same st, [dc in next st, 2 dc in next st] across, turn. *(50 dc)*

**Row 3:** Ch 3, [sk next st, **shell** *(see Special Stitch)* in next st] 23 times, sk next 2 sts, dc in last st, turn. *(23 shells, 2 dc)*

**Rows 4–10:** Ch 3, shell in ch sp of each shell across, dc in last st, turn.

**Rnd 11:** Now working in rnds, ch 1, sc in first st, 5 dc in next shell, [sc in next sp between shells, 5 dc in next shell] across, sc in last st, working in ends of rows, [ch 3, sc in next row] across to neck edge, sc in each st across neck edge, working down opposite edge, [ch 3, sc in next row] down, join in beg sc. Fasten off.

Sew rem button to top left neck edge using sp between sts for buttonhole.

## SCHOOL BAG

**Row 1:** With red, ch 15, sc in 2nd ch from hook and in each ch across to last ch, 2 sc in last ch, working on opposite side of starting ch, sc in each ch across, **do not join.** *(28 sc)*

*Note: Do not join or turn rounds. Mark first st of each rnd.*

**Rows 2–12:** Sc in each st around. Fasten off at end of last rnd.

## HANDLE

**Row 1:** Working on 1 side of Bag in 5 sts, join red with sc in first st, hdc in each of next 4 sts, turn. *(5 hdc)*

**Rows 2–28:** Ch 2, hdc in each st across, turn. Fasten off at end of last row.

Sew row 28 to 5 sts on opposite side of Bag. ■

# Winter Fun

DESIGNS BY **FRANCES HUGHES**

## SKILL LEVEL

EASY

## FINISHED SIZE
Fits 18-inch fashion doll

## MATERIALS
- Fine (sport) weight cotton yarn:
  5¼ oz/540 yds/150g burgundy
  3½ oz/350 yds/100g each pink
  and burgundy/variegated
- Bulky (chunky) weight eyelash yarn
  (1¾ oz/66 yds/50g per skein):
  2 skeins white
- Size F/5/3.75mm crochet hook
  or size needed to obtain gauge
- Sewing needle
- 18-inch Springfield doll
- 1 small snap
- Burgundy sewing thread

2 FINE

5 BULKY

## GAUGE
**With sport yarn:** 4 sts = 1 inch; 2 sc rows and
2 dc rows = 1 inch

## PATTERN NOTES
Join with slip stitch as indicated unless
otherwise stated.

Chain-3 at beginning of row or round counts as
first double crochet unless otherwise stated.

## INSTRUCTIONS
## LEGGINGS
## MAKE 2.
**Rnd 1:** With variegated, ch 18, **join** (*see Pattern
Notes*) in first ch to form ring, **ch 3** (*see Pattern
Notes*), dc in each ch around, join in 3rd ch of
beg ch-3. (*18 dc*)

**Rnds 2–21:** Ch 3, **bpdc** (*see Stitch Guide*) in next st, [**fpdc** (*see Stitch Guide*) in next st, bpdc in next st] around, join in 2nd ch of beg ch-2. Fasten off at end of last rnd.

Place on leg.

## SKIRT
**Row 1:** With burgundy, ch 43, sc in 2nd ch from hook and in each ch across, turn. *(42 dc)*

**Rows 2 & 3:** Ch 1, sc in each st across, turn.

**Row 4:** Ch 3, dc in same st, 2 dc in each st across, turn. *(84 dc)*

**Row 5:** Ch 1, working this row in **back lps** (*see Stitch Guide*), sc in each st across, turn.

**Row 6:** Ch 3, dc in same st, dc in next st, [2 dc in next st, dc in next st] across, turn. *(126 dc)*

**Row 7:** Working this row in back lps, ch 1, sc in each st across, turn.

**Row 8:** Ch 3, dc in each st across, turn.

**Rows 9–14:** [Rep rows 7 and 8 alternately] 3 times. Fasten off at end of last row.

**Row 15:** Join white with sc in first st on left edge, working left to right, for **reverse sc** (*see Stitch Guide*), insert hook in next st to the right, complete as sc, reverse sc in each st across. Fasten off.

Sew up back opening, leaving 2 inches at top waist edge unsewn.

Sew snap to waist at opening.

## PANTIES
**Row 1:** With pink, ch 43, sc in 2nd ch from hook and in each ch across, turn. *(42 sc)*

**Row 2:** Ch 1, sc in each st across, turn.

**Rows 3–10:** Ch 3, dc in each st across, turn. Fasten off at end of last row.

## CROTCH
**Row 1:** Join pink in 19th st, ch 3, dc in each of next 5 sts, turn. *(6 dc)*

**Rows 2–5:** Ch 3, dc in each st across, turn. Fasten off at end of last row.

Fold each side of Panties above crotch so ends meet at center of last row on Crotch, sew to crotch and sew seam at center back from Crotch to 1 inch from waist edge.

Sew snap to top back waist edge.

## JACKET
**Row 1:** With burgundy, ch 53, sc in 2nd ch from hook and in each ch across, turn. (52 sc)

**Rows 2 & 3:** Ch 1, sc in each st across, turn.

**Row 4:** Ch 3, dc in each st across, turn. (52 dc)

**Row 5:** Working this row in back lps, ch 1, sc in each st across, turn. *(52 sc)*

**Rows 6–9:** [Rep rows 4 and 5 alternately] twice.

**Row 10:** Rep row 5.

## FIRST FRONT
**Row 1:** Ch 1, sc in each of first 13 sts, leaving rem sts unworked, turn. (13 sc)

**Rows 2–10:** Ch 1, sc in each st across, turn. Fasten off at end of last row.

## CENTER BACK

**Row 1:** Sk next st on last row of Jacket, join burgundy with sc in next st, sc in next 23 sts, turn. (24 sc)

**Rows 2–10:** Ch 1, sc in each st across, turn. Fasten off at end of last row.

## 2ND FRONT

**Row 1:** Sk next st on last row of Jacket, join burgundy with sc in next st, sc in next 12 sts, turn. (13 sc)

**Rows 2–10:** Ch 1, sc in each st across, turn. Fasten off at end of last row.

Fold Fronts so edges meet Center Back at front and sew 6 sts on each Front and Back sides tog for shoulder seams.

## SLEEVES

**Rnd 1:** Join burgundy with sc at bottom of 1 armhole, evenly sp 21 more sc around armhole, **do not join.** (22 sc)

**Rnds 2–15:** Sc in each st around, join in beg sc. Fasten off at end of last rnd.

**Rnd 16:** Join white with sc in any st, sc in each st around, join in beg sc. Fasten off.

Rep on other armhole.

## COLLAR

**Row 1:** Working across neck edge with WS facing, join with sc in top right corner, sc in same st, evenly sp sc around neck edge ending with 2 sc in left top corner, turn.

**Rows 2–4:** Ch 1, sc in each st across, turn. Fasten off at end of last row.

## JACKET TRIM

Join white with sc in any st on Jacket, evenly sp sc around entire outer edge, join in beg sc. Fasten off.

Pull front corners down for lapels.

## HAT

**Rnd 1:** With burgundy, ch 4, join in beg ch to form ring, ch 3, 11 dc in ring, join in 3rd ch of beg ch-3. (12 dc)

**Rnd 2:** Ch 3, dc in same st, 2 dc in each st around, join in 3rd ch of beg ch-3. (24 dc)

**Rnd 3:** Ch 3, dc in same st, dc in next st, [2 dc in next st, dc in next st] around, join in 3rd ch of beg ch-3. (36 dc)

**Rnd 4:** Ch 3, dc in same st, dc in each of next 2 sts, [2 dc in next st, dc in each of next 2 sts] around, join in 3rd ch of beg ch-3. (48 dc)

**Rnd 5:** Ch 3, dc in each st around, join in 3rd ch of beg ch-3.

**Rnd 6:** Working this rnd in back lps, ch 1, sc in each st around, join in beg sc.

**Rnds 7–10:** [Rep rnds 5 and 6 alternately] twice.

**Rnd 11:** Ch 1, sc in each st around, join in beg sc. Fasten off.

## FLOWER

**Rnd 1:** With burgundy, ch 3, join in beg ch to form ring, ch 3, 11 dc in ring, join in 3rd ch of beg 3. Fasten off.

**Rnd 2:** Join white in first st, ch 3, dc in same st, 2 dc in each st around, join in 3rd ch of beg ch-3. Fasten off.

Tack Flower to side of Hat on row 9. ■

# Play Clothes

DESIGNS BY **SUE CHILDRESS**

## SKILL LEVEL

**EASY**

## FINISHED SIZE
Fits 18-inch fashion doll

## MATERIALS
- Katia Cotton Comfort fine (sport) weight yarn (1¾ oz/164 yds/50g per ball):
    1 ball each #17 orange and #30 blue
- Size F/5/3.75mm crochet hook or size needed to obtain gauge
- Sewing needle
- 1 pair Springfield Collection tennis shoes #5336
- 18-inch doll
- 7 novelty flower buttons
- Matching sewing thread

## GAUGE
9 dc = 2 inches; 4 dc rows = 1½ inches

## PATTERN NOTES
Join with slip stitch as indicated unless otherwise stated.

Chain-2 at beginning of row or round counts as first half double crochet unless otherwise stated.

Chain-3 at beginning of row or round counts as first double crochet unless otherwise stated.

## SPECIAL STITCH
**V-stitch (V-st):** (Dc, ch 1, dc) in indicted place.

## INSTRUCTIONS
### SHIRT
**Row 1:** With orange, ch 36, hdc in 3rd ch from hook (*first 2 chs count as first hdc*) and in each ch across, turn. (*35 hdc*)

**Row 2: Ch 2** (*see Pattern Notes*), hdc in same st, [hdc in each of next 2 sts, 2 hdc in next st] across, leaving last st unworked, turn. (*46 hdc*)

**Row 3:** Ch 2, hdc in same st, [hdc in each of next 3 sts, 2 hdc in next st] across, turn. (*57 hdc*)

**Row 4: Ch 3** (*see Pattern Notes*), dc in next st, [**V-st** (*see Special Stitch*) in next st, dc in each of next 2 sts] across, leaving rem st unworked, turn. (*38 dc, 18 V-sts*)

**Row 5:** Ch 3, dc in next st, [V-st in ch sp of next V-st, sk last dc of same V-st, dc in each of next 2 sts] 3 times, [4 dc in ch sp of next V-st, sk last dc of same V-st, dc in each of next 2 sts] 4 times, [V-st in ch sp of next V-st, sk last dc of same V-st, dc in each of next 2 sts] 4 times, [4 dc in ch sp of next V-st, sk last dc of same V-st, dc in each of next 2 sts] 4 times, [V-st in ch sp of next V-st, sk last dc of same V-st, dc in each of next 2 sts] 3 times, turn. (*70 dc, 10 V-sts*)

**Row 6:** Ch 3, dc in next st, [3 dc in ch sp of next V-st, sk last dc of same V-st, dc in each of next 2 dc] 3 times, sc in next st, [ch 3, sc in next st] 21 times, dc in each of next 2 sts, [3 dc in ch sp of next V-st, sk last dc of same V-st, dc in each of next 2 dc] 4 times, sc in next st, [ch 3, sc in next st] 21 times, dc in each of next 2 sts, [3 dc in ch sp of next V-st, sk last dc of same V-st, dc in each of next 2 dc] 3 times, turn. (*56 dc, 42 ch sps*)

**Row 7:** Ch 3, dc in each of next 16 sts, sc in next ch sp [ch 3, sc in next st] 20 times, dc in each of next 22 sts, sc in next ch sp, [ch 3, sc in next ch sp] 20 times, dc in each of last 17 sts, turn. (*56 dc, 40 ch sps*)

**Row 8:** Ch 3, dc in each of next 16 sts, ch 2, sk next 20 ch sps for sleeve, dc in each of next 22 sts, ch 2, sk next 20 ch sps for sleeve, dc in each of last 17 sts, turn. (*56 dc, 2 ch sps*)

**Row 9:** Ch 3, dc in each of next 16 sts, 2 tr in next ch sp, dc in each of next 22 sts, 2 tr in next ch sp, dc in each of last 17 sts, turn. (*56 dc, 4 tr*)

**Rows 10–12:** Ch 3, dc in each st across, turn. (*60 dc*)

**Row 13:** Ch 1, sc in first st, [ch 3, sc in next st] across, **do not turn**.

**Rnd 14:** Working in ends of rows, ch 1, 2 sc in first row, for **buttonhole**, ch 4, 2 sc in each of next 4 rows, for **buttonhole**, ch 4, 2 sc in each of next 5 rows, for **buttonhole**, ch 4, working in starting ch on opposite side of row 1, sc in first ch, [ch 3, sc in next ch] across, working in ends of rows, 2 sc in each row across, working in sts, sc in first st, [ch 3, sc in next st] across, **join** (*see Pattern Notes*) in beg sc. Fasten off.

Sew 3 buttons to side of front opposite buttonholes.

### SHORTS
**Row 1:** With blue, ch 60, hdc in 3rd ch from hook and in each ch across, turn. (*59 hdc*)

**Rows 2–10:** Ch 2, hdc in each st across, turn.

### CROTCH
**Row 1:** Sl st in each of first 23 sts, ch 2, hdc in each of next 13 sts, leaving rem sts unworked, turn. (*14 hdc*)

**Rows 2–7:** Ch 2, hdc in each st across, turn. Fasten off at end of last row.

Fold each side of Shorts above crotch so ends meet at center of last row on Crotch, sew in place.

### FIRST LEG
**Rnd 1:** Join blue in any st on 1 leg opening, ch 2, evenly sp 35 more hdc around opening, join in 2nd ch of beg ch-2. (*36 hdc*)

**Rnd 2:** Ch 2, hdc in each st around, join in 2nd ch of beg ch-2. Fasten off.

**Rnd 3:** Join orange with sc in first st, ch 3, [sc in next st, ch 3] around, join in beg sc. Fasten off.

Rep on other leg opening.

Sew 1 button to top left back opening, using spaces between sts on top right opening as button holes.

## SHOELACE
**MAKE 2.**
With 2 strands orange held tog as 1, ch 65. Fasten off.

Lace 1 in each shoe.

## HAT
**Rnd 1:** With blue, ch 6, join in beg ch to form ring, ch 2, 11 hdc in ring, join in 2nd ch of beg ch-2. *(12 hdc)*

**Rnd 2:** Sl st in next st, ch 2, hdc in same st, 2 hdc in each st around including sk st, join in 2nd ch of beg ch-2. *(24 hdc)*

*Note: For rnds 3–7, sk first st, start rnd in 2nd st. At end of rnd, work in first sk st.*

**Rnd 3:** Sl st in next st, ch 3, dc in same st, dc in next st, [2 dc in next st, dc in next st] around, join in 3rd ch of beg ch-3. *(36 dc)*

**Rnd 4:** Sl st in next st, ch 3, dc in each of next 2 sts, 2 dc in next st, [dc in each of next 3 sts, 2 dc in next st] around, join in 3rd ch of beg ch-3. *(45 dc)*

**Rnd 5:** Sl st in next st, ch 3, dc in same st, dc in each of next 4 sts, [2 dc in next st, dc in each of next 4 sts] around, join in 3rd ch of beg ch-3. *(54 dc)*

**Rnds 6 & 7:** Sl st in next st, ch 3, dc in each st around, join in 3rd ch of beg ch-3. Fasten off at end of last rnd.

**Rnd 8:** Join orange with sc in any dc, ch 3, [sc in next st, ch 3] around, join in beg sc. Fasten off.

Sew 3 buttons to top side of Hat. ∎

# Dress Up

## DESIGNS BY **FRANCES HUGHES**

### SKILL LEVEL

**EASY**

### FINISHED SIZE
Fits 18-inch fashion doll

### MATERIALS
- Louisa Harding Jasmine fine (sport) weight yarn (1¾ oz/107 yds/50g per ball):
    3 balls #18 plume
- Fine (sport) weight cotton yarn:
    2 oz/200 yds/57g white
- Sizes F/5/3.75mm and G/6/4mm crochet hooks or size needed to obtain gauge
- Sewing needle
- White ribbon:
    ⅜-inch wide: 1 yd
    ⅛-inch wide: 1 yd
- 18-inch Springfield doll
- 3 small snaps
- Matching sewing thread

### GAUGE
**Size F hook:** 5 dc = 1 inch

### PATTERN NOTES
Join with slip stitch as indicated unless otherwise stated.

Chain-3 at beginning of row or round counts as first double crochet unless otherwise stated.

Chain-4 at beginning of row or round counts as first treble crochet unless otherwise stated.

### INSTRUCTIONS
### DRESS
**Row 1:** With size F hook and plume, ch 47, sc in 2nd ch from hook and in each ch across, turn. (46 sc)

**Rows 2–6:** Ch 1, sc in each st across, turn.

## FIRST BACK

**Row 1:** Ch 1, sc in each of first 11 sts, leaving rem sts unworked, turn. *(11 sc)*

**Rows 2–9:** Ch 1, sc in each st across, turn.

**Row 10:** For **shoulder,** ch 1, sc in each of first 7 sts, leaving rem sts unworked, turn.

**Rows 11–13:** Ch 1, sc in each st across, turn. Fasten off at end of last row.

## FRONT

**Row 1:** Sk next st on row 6 of Dress, join plume with sc in next st, sc in each of next 21 sts, leaving rem sts unworked, turn. *(22 sc).*

**Rows 2–13:** Ch 1, sc in each st across, turn.

## FIRST FRONT SHOULDER

**Row 1:** Ch 1, sc in each of first 7 sts, leaving rem sts unworked, turn *(7 sc)*

**Rows 2–6:** Ch 1, sc in each st across, turn. Fasten off at end of last row.

## 2ND FRONT SHOULDER

**Row 1:** Sk next 8 sts on last row of Front, join with sc in next st, sc in each of last 6 sts turn. *(7 sc)*

**Rows 2–6:** Ch 1, sc in each st across, turn. Fasten off at end of last row.

## 2ND BACK

**Row 1:** Sk next st on row 6 of Dress, join plume with sc in next st, sc in each of last 10 sts, turn. *(11 sts)*

**Rows 2–9:** Ch 1, sc in each st across, turn. Fasten off at end of last row.

**Row 10:** For **neck,** sk first 4 sts, join with sc in next st, for **shoulder,** sc in last 6 sts, turn. *(7 sts)*

**Rows 11–13:** Ch 1, sc in each st across, turn. Fasten off at end of last row.

Sew shoulder seams.

## SLEEVES

**Rnd 1:** With size F hook and plume, join with sc in sk st at bottom of 1 armhole, sc in end of each of next 4 rows, hdc in end of each of next 3 rows, dc in end of each of next 2 rows, 2 dc in end of each of next 8 rows, dc in end of each of next 2 rows, hdc in end of each of next 3 rows, sc in end of each of next 4 rows, **join** *(see Pattern Notes)* in beg sc. *(35 sts)*

**Rnds 2–4:** **Ch 3** *(see Pattern Notes)*, dc in each st around, join in 3rd ch of beg ch-3.

**Rnd 5:** Ch 1, sc in first st, [**sc dec** *(see Stitch Guide)* in next 2 sts] around, join in beg sc. *(18 sc)*

**Rnd 6:** Ch 1, sc in each st around, join in beg sc. Fasten off.

**Rnd 7:** With size F hook and white, join in bottom underarm st, ch 3, [sl st in next st, ch 3] around, join in beg sc. Fasten off.

Rep on other armhole.

## NECK TRIM

**Row 1:** With WS facing and size F hook and plume, join with sc in top right corner, evenly sp 31 sc across neck edge to top left corner, turn. *(32 sc)*

**Row 2:** Ch 1, sc in each st across. Fasten off.

**Row 3:** With size F hook and white, join in first st, [ch 3, sl st in next st] across. Fasten off.

## SKIRT

**Row 1:** Working in starting ch on opposite side of row 1, with size F hook and plume, join in beg ch, ch 3, dc in same ch, 2 dc in each st across, turn. (92 dc)

**Rows 2–12:** Ch 3, dc in each st across, turn.

**Row 13:** **Ch 4** *(see Pattern Notes)*, 2 tr in next st, [tr in next st, 2 tr in next st] across, turn. Fasten off.

**Row 14:** Join white in first st, [ch 3, sl st in next st] across. Fasten off.

With matching colors, sew back seam, leaving 1½ inches at waist edge unsewn.

## FINISHING

**1.** Sew 1 snap at waist edge and 1 at neck edge.

**2.** Cut 3 lengths of ⅛-inch ribbon, each 12 inches long. Tie each length into a bow with knots in ribbon ends. Tack 1 bow to top of each Sleeve and 1 at center front neck.

**3.** Cut 3 lengths of ⅜-inch ribbon, each 12 inches long. Set 1 aside. Fold 1 end of 1 piece of ribbon under ¼ inch and tack to waist edge on 1 side of Back. Rep on other side of Back with other strand of ribbon. Pull rem ends of ribbon to center front and tie ends into a bow. Tie knot in each ribbon end.

## PANTIES

**Row 1:** With size F hook and plume, ch 43, sc in 2nd ch from hook and in each ch across, turn. *(42 sc)*

**Row 2:** Ch 1, sc in each st across, turn.

**Rows 3–10:** Ch 3, dc in each st across, turn. Fasten off at end of last row. *(42 dc)*

## CROTCH

**Row 1:** Join plume in 19th st, ch 3, dc in each of next 5 sts, leaving rem sts unworked, turn. *(6 sc)*

**Rows 2–5:** Ch 3, dc in each st across, turn. Fasten off at end of last row.

Fold each side of Panties above crotch so ends meet at center of last row on Crotch, sew to Crotch and sew seam at center back from Crotch to 1 inch from waist edge.

Sew snap to top back waist edge.

## LEG

**Rnd 1:** Join plume with sc in any st on 1 leg opening, evenly sp 27 more sc around opening, join in beg sc. Fasten off. *(28 sc)*

**Rnd 2:** Join white in first sc, ch 3, [sl st in next st, ch 3] around, join in beg sl st. Fasten off.

Rep on other leg opening.

## HAT

**Rnd 1:** With size F hook and plume, ch 4, join in beg ch to form ring, ch 3, 11 dc in ring, join in 3rd ch of beg ch-3. *(12 dc)*

**Rnd 2:** Ch 3, dc in same st, 2 dc in each st around, join in 3rd ch of beg ch-3. *(24 dc)*

**Rnd 3:** Ch 3, dc in same st, dc in next st, [2 dc in next st, dc in next st] around, join in 3rd ch of beg ch-3. *(36 dc)*

**Rnd 4:** Ch 3, dc in same st, dc in each of next 2 sts, [2 dc in next st, dc in each of next 2 sts] around, join in 3rd ch of beg ch-3. *(48 dc)*

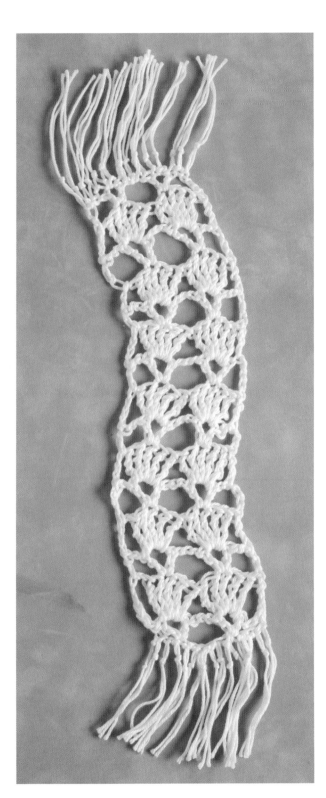

**Rnds 5–8:** Ch 3, dc in each st around, join in 3rd ch of beg ch-3.

**Rnds 9 & 10:** Ch 1, sc in each st around, join in beg sc.

**Rnd 11:** Ch 4 *(counts as first tr)*, tr in same st, tr in next st, [2 tr in next st, tr in next st] around, join in 4th ch of beg ch-4. Fasten off. *(72 tr)*

**Rnd 12:** Join white in first st, ch 3, [sl st in next st, ch 3] around, join in beg sl st. Fasten of.

Tie rem ⅜-ribbon length into a bow; tie ribbon ends into knots. Tack to Hat on rnds 9 and 10.

## STOLE
**Row 1:** With size G hook and white, ch 16, (dc, ch 2, dc) in 8th ch from hook *(first 6 chs count as first tr and ch-2 sp)*, ch 3, sk next 4 chs, (dc, ch 2, dc) in next ch, ch 2, tr in last ch, turn. *(4 dc, 4 ch-2 sps, 2 tr, 1 ch-3 sp)*

**Row 2:** Ch 4, sk first ch-2 sp, 5 tr in next ch-2 sp, sk next ch-3 sp, 5 tr in next ch-2 sp, tr in last st, turn. *(12 tr)*

**Row 3:** Ch 6 *(counts as first tr and ch-2 sp)*, sk first 2 tr, (dc, ch 2, dc) in next st, ch 3, sk next 4 tr, (dc, ch 2, dc) in next tr, ch 2, tr in last st, turn. *(4 dc, 4 ch-2 sps, 2 tr, 1 ch-3 sp)*

**Rows 4–15:** [Rep rows 2 and 3 alternately] 6 times. Fasten off at end of last row.

## FRINGE
For each Fringe, cut strand white 3 inches long. Fold strand in half, insert hook in st or sp, pull fold through, pull all loose ends through fold, tighten. Trim. Tie knot in ends ¼ inch from fold.

Attach 16 Fringe evenly spaced across each short end of Stole. ■

# STITCH GUIDE

## STITCH ABBREVIATIONS

beg .............................. begin/begins/beginning
bpdc .............................. back post double crochet
bpsc .............................. back post single crochet
bptr .............................. back post treble crochet
CC .............................. contrasting color
ch(s) .............................. chain(s)
ch- .............................. refers to chain or space
previously made (i.e., ch-1 space)
ch sp(s) .............................. chain space(s)
cl(s) .............................. cluster(s)
cm .............................. centimeter(s)
dc .............................. double crochet (singular/plural)
dc dec .............................. double crochet 2 or more
stitches together, as indicated
dec .............................. decrease/decreases/decreasing
dtr .............................. double treble crochet
ext .............................. extended
fpdc .............................. front post double crochet
fpsc .............................. front post single crochet
fptr .............................. front post treble crochet
g .............................. gram(s)
hdc .............................. half double crochet
hdc dec .............................. half double crochet 2 or more
stitches together, as indicated
inc .............................. increase/increases/increasing
lp(s) .............................. loop(s)
MC .............................. main color
mm .............................. millimeter(s)
oz .............................. ounce(s)
pc .............................. popcorn(s)
rem .............................. remain/remains/remaining
rep(s) .............................. repeat(s)
rnd(s) .............................. round(s)
RS .............................. right side
sc .............................. single crochet (singular/plural)
sc dec .............................. single crochet 2 or more
stitches together, as indicated
sk .............................. skip/skipped/skipping
sl st(s) .............................. slip stitch(es)
sp(s) .............................. space(s)/spaced
st(s) .............................. stitch(es)
tog .............................. together
tr .............................. treble crochet
trtr .............................. triple treble
WS .............................. wrong side
yd(s) .............................. yard(s)
yo .............................. yarn over

## YARN CONVERSION

| OUNCES TO GRAMS | | GRAMS TO OUNCES | |
|---|---|---|---|
| 1 | 28.4 | 25 | ⅞ |
| 2 | 56.7 | 40 | 1⅔ |
| 3 | 85.0 | 50 | 1¾ |
| 4 | 113.4 | 100 | 3½ |

| UNITED STATES | | UNITED KINGDOM |
|---|---|---|
| sl st (slip stitch) | = | sc (single crochet) |
| sc (single crochet) | = | dc (double crochet) |
| hdc (half double crochet) | = | htr (half treble crochet) |
| dc (double crochet) | = | tr (treble crochet) |
| tr (treble crochet) | = | dtr (double treble crochet) |
| dtr (double treble crochet) | = | ttr (triple treble crochet) |
| skip | = | miss |

**Reverse Single Crochet (reverse sc):** Ch 1. Skip first st. [Working from left to right, insert hook in next st from front to back, draw up lp on hook, yo, and draw through both lps on hook.]

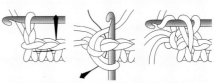

**Chain (ch):** Yo, pull through lp on hook.

**Single crochet (sc):** Insert hook in st, yo, pull through st, yo, pull through both lps on hook.

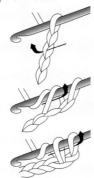

**Double crochet (dc):** Yo, insert hook in st, yo, pull through st, [yo, pull through 2 lps] twice.

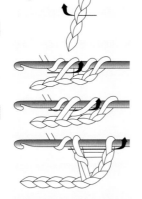

**Single crochet decrease (sc dec):** (Insert hook, yo, draw lp through) in each of the sts indicated, yo, draw through all lps on hook.

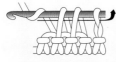

Example of 2-sc dec

**Half double crochet decrease (hdc dec):** (Yo, insert hook, yo, draw lp through) in each of the sts indicated, yo, draw through all lps on hook.

Example of 2-hdc dec

**Front loop (front lp) Back loop (back lp)**

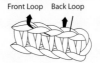

Front Loop    Back Loop

**Front post stitch (fp): Back post stitch (bp):** When working post st, insert hook from right to left around post st on previous row.

Back    Front
Post of Stitch

**Half double crochet (hdc):** Yo, insert hook in st, yo, pull through st, yo, pull through all 3 lps on hook.

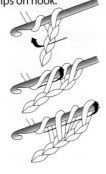

**Double treble crochet (dtr):** Yo 3 times, insert hook in st, yo, pull through st, [yo, pull through 2 lps] 4 times.

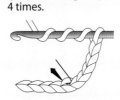

**Double crochet decrease (dc dec):** Yo, insert hook, yo, draw loop through, yo, draw through 2 lps on hook) in each of the sts indicated, yo, draw through all lps on hook.

Example of 2-dc dec

**Slip stitch (sl st):** Insert hook in st, pull through both lps on hook.

**Chain Color Change (ch color change)** Yo with new color, draw through last lp on hook.

**Double Crochet Color Change (dc color change)** Drop first color, yo with new color, draw through last 2 lps of st.

**Treble crochet (tr):** Yo twice, insert hook in st, yo, pull through st, [yo, pull through 2 lps] 3 times.

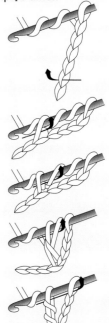

**Treble crochet decrease (tr dec):** Holding back last lp of each st, tr in each of the sts indicated, yo, pull through all lps on hook.

Example of 2-tr dec

# Metric
## Conversion
## Charts

### METRIC CONVERSIONS

| | | | | |
|---|---|---|---|---|
| yards | x | .9144 | = | metres (m) |
| yards | x | 91.44 | = | centimetres (cm) |
| inches | x | 2.54 | = | centimetres (cm) |
| inches | x | 25.40 | = | millimetres (mm) |
| inches | x | .0254 | = | metres (m) |

| | | | | |
|---|---|---|---|---|
| centimetres | x | .3937 | = | inches |
| metres | x | 1.0936 | = | yards |

### INCHES INTO MILLIMETRES & CENTIMETRES (Rounded off slightly)

| inches | mm | cm | inches | cm | inches | cm | inches | cm |
|---|---|---|---|---|---|---|---|---|
| 1/8 | 3 | 0.3 | 5 | 12.5 | 21 | 53.5 | 38 | 96.5 |
| 1/4 | 6 | 0.6 | 5 1/2 | 14 | 22 | 56 | 39 | 99 |
| 3/8 | 10 | 1 | 6 | 15 | 23 | 58.5 | 40 | 101.5 |
| 1/2 | 13 | 1.3 | 7 | 18 | 24 | 61 | 41 | 104 |
| 5/8 | 15 | 1.5 | 8 | 20.5 | 25 | 63.5 | 42 | 106.5 |
| 3/4 | 20 | 2 | 9 | 23 | 26 | 66 | 43 | 109 |
| 7/8 | 22 | 2.2 | 10 | 25.5 | 27 | 68.5 | 44 | 112 |
| 1 | 25 | 2.5 | 11 | 28 | 28 | 71 | 45 | 114.5 |
| 1 1/4 | 32 | 3.2 | 12 | 30.5 | 29 | 73.5 | 46 | 117 |
| 1 1/2 | 38 | 3.8 | 13 | 33 | 30 | 76 | 47 | 119.5 |
| 1 3/4 | 45 | 4.5 | 14 | 35.5 | 31 | 79 | 48 | 122 |
| 2 | 50 | 5 | 15 | 38 | 32 | 81.5 | 49 | 124.5 |
| 2 1/2 | 65 | 6.5 | 16 | 40.5 | 33 | 84 | 50 | 127 |
| 3 | 75 | 7.5 | 17 | 43 | 34 | 86.5 | | |
| 3 1/2 | 90 | 9 | 18 | 46 | 35 | 89 | | |
| 4 | 100 | 10 | 19 | 48.5 | 36 | 91.5 | | |
| 4 1/2 | 115 | 11.5 | 20 | 51 | 37 | 94 | | |

### KNITTING NEEDLES CONVERSION CHART

| Canada/U.S. | 0 | 1 | 2 | 3 | 4 | 5 | 6 | 7 | 8 | 9 | 10 | 10½ | 11 | 13 | 15 |
|---|---|---|---|---|---|---|---|---|---|---|---|---|---|---|---|
| Metric (mm) | 2 | 2¼ | 2¾ | 3¼ | 3½ | 3¾ | 4 | 4½ | 5 | 5½ | 6 | 6½ | 8 | 9 | 10 |

### CROCHET HOOKS CONVERSION CHART

| Canada/U.S. | 1/B | 2/C | 3/D | 4/E | 5/F | 6/G | 8/H | 9/I | 10/J | 10½/K | N |
|---|---|---|---|---|---|---|---|---|---|---|---|
| Metric (mm) | 2.25 | 2.75 | 3.25 | 3.5 | 3.75 | 4.25 | 5 | 5.5 | 6 | 6.5 | 9.0 |

*Dress-Up Fashions for 18" Dolls* is published by DRG, 306 East Parr Road, Berne, IN 46711. Printed in USA. Copyright © 2010 DRG.

**RETAIL STORES:** If you would like to carry this pattern book or any other DRG publications, visit DRGwholesale.com.

Every effort has been made to ensure that the instructions in this publication are complete and accurate.
We cannot, however, take responsibility for human error, typographical mistakes or variations in individual work.
Please visit AnniesCustomerCare.com to check for pattern updates.

ISBN: 978-1-59635-318-3                                                                                                    5 6 7 8 9